**CHRIS &
MATHILD
STUART**

T0352538

50

On track

Quick ID guide to southern
and East African animal tracks

Published by Struik Nature
(an imprint of Penguin Random House SA (Pty) Ltd)
Reg. No. 1953/000441/07
The Estuaries No 4, Oxbow Crescent,
Century Avenue, Century City, 7441
PO Box 1144, Cape Town, 8000 South Africa

www.penguinrandomhouse.co.za

First published in 2013
10 9 8 7 6

Publisher: Pippa Parker
Managing editor: Helen de Villiers
Editor: Lisa Delaney
Designer: Janice Evans

Reproduction by Hirt & Carter Cape (Pty) Ltd
Printed and bound by DJE Flexible Print Solutions, South Africa

ISBN 978 1 92057 253 2 (PRINT)
ISBN 978 1 77584 053 4 (EPUB)
ISBN 978 1 77584 052 7 (PDF)

Contents

Introduction

This guide will help you ease your way into identifying the animal tracks you may encounter on your wanderings. Some locations are more suited to finding clear tracks than others. Prime sites include damp silt, clay and fine sand around dam edges, river banks, temporary rain-filled pools and the area between high and low tides on coastal beaches.

For each species in this guide, you will find a 'perfect' drawing of a front and back track and, for most tracks, a photograph, too. We say 'perfect' because the clear track is often the exception and many tracks you encounter will be blurred, smudged or distorted. But do not be discouraged – if you follow the animal's line of travel, you are likely to encounter one or more clear footprints.

Knowledge of reading tracks, apart from being a useful tool for hunter, farmer and scientist, can also be a pleasure, adding a new dimension to hikes and wanderings. Even from your vehicle, larger tracks are often visible on roads and verges within game parks.

When on foot and tracking in big game country, always be alert and aware of the potential dangers.

How to use this guide

● First refer to the simplified track key (inside cover) and find the track that most closely fits the footprint you are trying to identify. This will direct you to the appropriate section in the book

● It is always good to have an idea of what species occur in the area, as this helps to narrow down your choices. For example, you will not encounter lion tracks in the Tankwa Karoo, but you may find leopard footprints. However, in the Karoo National Park you may encounter both. Also bear in mind that, on private game farms, you may encounter the tracks of species far outside their natural range, especially in southern Africa.

● Try to look for several tracks, as this may help you build up a clearer picture, especially in loose or coarse soil. Walk up and down the side of the trail and not directly on it, in case you need to backtrack.

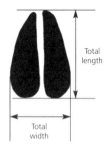

● Track into the sun wherever possible, as this helps to make the track more visible. Early mornings and late afternoons are best.

● When following tracks, you need to look not only straight down, but also to scan several metres ahead of you – this may make a track more visible than when you are on top of it.

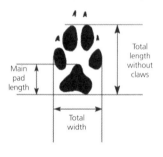

● It is always a good idea to photograph clear tracks and, in this way, build up a personal reference collection. Always use a scale in your photographs, or take accurate measurements.

The drawings on the left of this page show you which measurements are the most important. In general, with paw tracks where claws are present, the claw lengths are excluded from the measurement. This is because claw lengths may vary considerably, even within the same species.

● The **stride** is the distance between the individual tracks; the **straddle** is the distance between tracks to the left and right of the animal as it walks, trots or gallops.

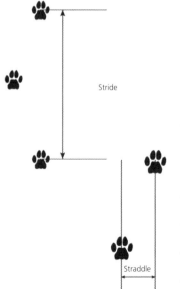

● Always be alert for other traces and signs associated with the tracks you are attempting to identify. Droppings, evidence of feeding and scratch marks on the ground or on trees may help you to identify a species.

GOOD TRACKING!

Heavyweights

Just four species fall into this category, all of which have large feet to support their substantial bulk. Tracks of elephant, hippo and rhino are easily distinguished from one another. The two rhinoceros species are a little more difficult, but can usually be separated based on the habitats they occupy. In both regions all four species are mainly restricted to conservation areas.

Savanna elephant

Right front

Right back

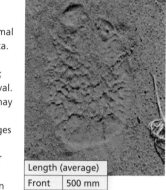

- Largest animal tracks in Africa. Front tracks almost round; back tracks oval. Fresh tracks may show clear mosaic of ridges and furrows.
- In groups or solitary bulls.
- Principally in savanna.

Length (average)	
Front	500 mm
Back	500 mm

Hippopotamus

Right front

Right back

- Only track of its kind in these regions, with four obvious toes on each foot. Has a wide track straddle – the trails used by these semi-amphibious animals show a distinct pair of shallow trenches.
- Usually associated with water, but tracks may be encountered on distant grazing grounds.

Length (average)	
Front	250 mm
Back	210 mm

5

Square-lipped (White) rhinoceros

Right front

Right back

- Of the two rhinos, the square-lipped species has the larger tracks.
- Three horny-nailed toes, largest in front, smaller, ones on either side. Hind tracks narrower than front. Indentation on posterior edge usually more pronounced than in black rhinos.
- More open grassland areas than black rhinos.

Length (average)	
Front	300 mm
Back	280 mm

Hook-lipped (Black) rhinoceros

Right front

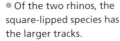

Right back

- Three horny-nailed toes, same conformation as white rhinos. Indentation on posterior edge usually not clearly defined. Fresh tracks of both rhinos may show mosaic of cracks in fine soil.
- Tracks are more likely to be found in densely bushed areas, but there are exceptions.

Length (average)	
Front	200 mm
Back	180 mm

Cloven hooves

This large group of mammals includes the antelope, but also pigs, cattle, sheep and goats. All walk on the tips of third and fourth toes; each is capped by a horny sheath. Each hoof consists of two more-or-less equal halves; the front track is usually slightly larger than the back.

Giraffe

Right front

Right back

- Largest hooves of any mammal in these regions. Anterior hoof edge usually rounded or squared off.
- Solitary or in small groups.

Length (average)	
Front	180 mm
Back	170 mm

Buffalo

Right front

Right back

- Large size; similar to cattle, eland. Dewclaws (false hooves) may leave indentations in soft mud.
- In small to large herds or solitary bulls.
- Mainly conservation areas in wooded grassland.

Length (average)	
Front	120 mm
Back	120 mm

Nigel Dennis / IOA

Eland

Right front

Right back

- Cow-like tracks, similar in size to those of buffaloes.
- Obviously rounded anterior edges.
- Usually found in herds in conservation areas.
- Wooded savanna.

Length (average)	
Front	100 mm
Back	85 mm

Sitatunga

Right front

Right back

Length (average)	
Front	150 mm
Back	80 mm

- Tracks uniquely shaped – long and splayed. Front tracks much longer than back.
- Solitary and small groups, very habitat restricted.
- Swamps.

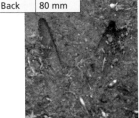

Waterbuck

Right front

Right back

- Large, fairly sharply pointed, heart-shaped tracks.
- Similar to oryx tracks, but different habitats.
- Herds, small groups, or solitary individuals.
- Grassy woods.

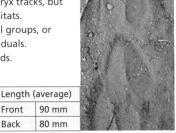

Length (average)	
Front	90 mm
Back	80 mm

Oryx (Gemsbok in SA)

Right front

Right back

- Large, heart-shaped tracks. Dewclaws may leave marks in soft soil or sand.
- Herds and solitary.
- Desert and semi-desert areas.

Length (average)	
Front	110 mm
Back	105 mm

Hartebeest

Right front

Right back

- Large size; inner edges of hooves are usually concave and may show in track.
- In herds; bulls may be solitary.
- Open savanna grassland and woodland; also semi-desert.

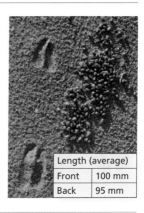

Length (average)	
Front	100 mm
Back	95 mm

Blue wildebeest (White-bearded in EA)

Right front

Right back

- Large tracks; in soft ground, marks left by dewclaws are common.
- Herding antelope, sometimes found in large numbers.
- Open grassland and woodland savanna.

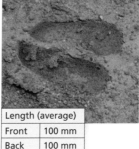

Length (average)	
Front	100 mm
Back	100 mm

Black wildebeest

Right front

Right back

- Similar to tracks of blue wildebeest, but smaller on average.
- Small to large herds, only in conservation areas.
- Central South African plains only, but widely introduced in SA and Namibia.

Length (average)	
Front	100 mm
Back	90 mm

Roan antelope

Length (average)	
Front	120 mm
Back	120 mm

Right front

Right back

- Large size; may be confused with sable or eland.
- Small herds and solitary bulls.
- Rare; mainly in conservation areas.
- Open or lightly wooded grassland.

Sable antelope

Right front

Right back

- Similar to Roan, but Roan's anterior edge is usually more pointed (although not a hard-and-fast rule).
- Herds and lone bulls.
- Rare; mainly in conservation areas.
- Open woodland.

Length (average)	
Front	110 mm
Back	104 mm

Greater kudu

Right front

Right back

- Relatively small tracks for their size.
- Tracks typically oval.
- Common and widespread.
- Small herds or solitary.
- Wooded savanna and hill country.

Length (average)	
Front	67 mm
Back	56 mm

Bushpig

Right front

Right back

Track with dewclaws

- Medium-sized; dewclaws leave obvious marks in soft mud (see third drawing).
- Much 'ploughing' of ground when foraging, and massed tracks can be confusing; signs of feeding aid identification.
- Usually in groups (sounders) of 4–10 individuals.
- Forest, woodland and dense thickets, usually near water.

Length (average)	
Front	60 mm
Back	53 mm

Nigel Dennis / IOA

Warthog

Right front

Right back

- Relatively small, rounded and 'dainty' hooves that leave distinctive tracks.
- Live in groups, though boars are solitary.
- Also look for characteristic droppings in favoured feeding areas.
- Open country, but also lightly wooded areas with abundant grasses.

Length (average)	
Front	48 mm
Back	47 mm

Impala

Right front

Right back

- Rather delicate, heart-shaped tracks.
- Usually in large numbers on favoured feeding grounds.
- Open and wooded savanna, but rarely open grassland.

Length (average)	
Front	47 mm
Back	46 mm

12

Springbok

Right front

Right back

- Neat, heart-shaped tracks that come to a sharp point.
- Mainly medium to large herds, and tracks are often massed; solitary males may also be encountered.
- Only in southern Africa: desert and semi-desert; farms.

Length (average)	
Front	55 mm
Back	54 mm

Grant's gazelle

Right front

Right back

- Neat and compact tracks.
- Solitary rams and small herds.
- Semi-desert scrub to open savanna woodland
- Restricted to East Africa

Length (average)	
Front	55 mm
Back	54 mm

Thomson's gazelle

Right front

Right back

- Small, fairly slender tracks.
- Small herds to 60 animals; large aggregations.
- Mainly Serengeti and the Mara; not found in southern Africa.
- Open savanna grassland.

Length (average)	
Front	45 mm
Back	43 mm

Blesbok & Bontebok

Right front

Right back

- These two subspecies have near identical hooves.
- Blesbok in herds, bontebok in smaller groups.
- Blesbok in open central plains of inner SA; bontebok in Cape heathland. Both absent from East Africa.

Length (average)	
Front	62 mm
Back	63 mm

Bushbuck

Right front

Right back

- Neat, oval-shaped tracks.
- Solitary, but tracks may be abundant in areas of high density.
- Occurs widely in both regions.
- Forest, woodland and thicket.

Length (average)	
Front	50 mm
Back	44 mm

Nyala

Right front

Right back

- Similar tracks to bushbuck, but slightly larger.
- Small groups and solitary rams.
- Found only in east of southern Africa; introduced to game farms elsewhere.
- Dry woodland.

Length (average)	
Front	57 mm
Back	53 mm

Common reedbuck

Right front

Right back

- Fairly long tracks that resemble the smaller steenbok.
- Solitary and small groups; may reach high densities in prime habitat.
- River floodplains, reed beds, flooded grassland.

Length (average)	
Front	65 mm
Back	61 mm

Common duiker

Right front

Right back

- Small, compact, heart-shaped tracks.
- Solitary; never in groups.
- Prefer scrub and bush thickets in low to high rainfall areas.

Length (average)	
Front	40 mm
Back	42 mm

Steenbok

Right front

Right back

- Small, elegant tracks; narrow and pointed anterior edge.
- Widespread in suitable habitat throughout regions, including farmland.
- Open country with some brush or grass cover.

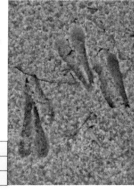

Length (average)	
Front	38 mm
Back	40 mm

Grysbok

Right front

Right back

- Small, neat, heart-shaped tracks. Those of Sharpe's and Cape are identical, but tracks of Cape are larger.
- Cape in southwest, Sharpe's in northeast.
- Low thicket, thick scrub brush and open glades.

Length (average)	
Front	34 mm
Back	35 mm

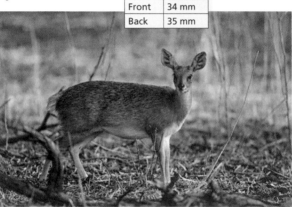

Nigel Dennis / IOA

Klipspringer

Right front

Right back

- Tracks consist of two neat oval 'slots' made only by tips of hooves.
- Usually 2–4 animals in family unit.
- Widespread, but patchy range.
- Rocky outcrops, hill and mountain ranges.

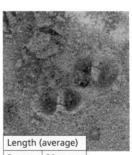

Length (average)	
Front	20 mm
Back	21 mm

16

Paws

Paws range in size from the substantial span of the lion's paw to the delicate rosette of the banded mongoose's, and can be divided into two broad groups: paws without claws showing in the track (includes all of the cats, except the cheetah, and the genets) and paws with claw impressions (includes members of the dog family, mongooses, hyaenas and civet, amongst others). Cats have a distinctive double indentation on the anterior main pad edge, which is lacking in other groups.

Lion

Right front

Right back

- Largest of the cat tracks, with large toe pads; front pad track is larger than that of back. Has a distinctive double indentation on back edge of main pad.
- Live in groups, or prides, of 2–30 individuals.
- Savanna types, but wide tolerance.

Length (average)	
Front	128 mm
Back	121 mm

Leopard

Right front

Right back

- Similar to lion tracks, but smaller; front tracks are rounder. Double indentation on the back edge of the main pads.
- Solitary for much of their lives; except for females and their cubs.
- Make regular use of trails and roads.
- Widespread and in most major habitat types.

Length (average)	
Front	92 mm
Back	92 mm

Caracal

Right front

Right back

- Typical cat tracks with double indentation on back edge of main pads.
- Solitary.
- Will use paths and roadways.
- Wide distribution.

Length (average)	
Front	47 mm
Back	55 mm

Serval

Right front

Right back

- Tracks are more rounded and compact than those of the similar-sized caracal.
- Solitary.
- Grassland.

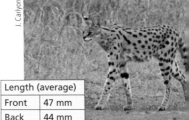

J. Carlyon

Length (average)	
Front	47 mm
Back	44 mm

Wildcat

Right front

Right back

- Identical to domestic cat tracks, but larger. Typical double indentation on back edge of main pads.
- Solitary.
- Diverse habitats.

Length (average)	
Front	36 mm
Back	36 mm

Genets

Right front

Right back

- Similar to cat tracks, but main pad indentations obscure.
- Several species occur in both regions.
- Occupy most habitats.

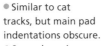

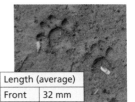

Length (average)	
Front	32 mm
Back	30 mm

Spotted hyaena

Right front

- Front tracks larger than back. Angled back edge on main pads. Large toe pads (close to main pads) clearly show in tracks.
- Live in packs of 3–15 or more, but solitary individuals may be encountered.
- Widespread but in south mainly restricted to conservation areas.
- Open country, but also rocky hilly areas and woodland.

Right back

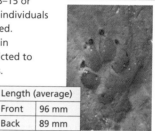

Length (average)	
Front	96 mm
Back	89 mm

Brown hyaena

Right front

- Similar to the tracks of spotted hyaenas, but back tracks are proportionally smaller. Slanting back edge of main pads; large toe pads close to main pads.
- Live in clan units; solitary foragers.
- In southern African conservation areas and on farms; similar tracks to those of striped hyaena of East Africa.

Right back

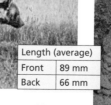

A. Weaving

Length (average)	
Front	89 mm
Back	66 mm

Cheetah

Right front

Right back

- Only cats with claw marks in tracks. Double-indentation on back edge of main pads; toe pads smaller than those of other big cats.
- Found in groups of 1–5, but often solitary.
- Open savanna.

Length (average)	
Front	84 mm
Back	80 mm

African wild dog

Right front

Right back

A. Stein

- Typical dog tracks: near-triangular main pads, fairly large toe pads. Smaller tracks than those of hyaenas; front paws notably larger than those of jackals. Claw marks usually clear.
- Live in packs; highly mobile.
- Open country.

Length (average)	
Front	76 mm
Back	68 mm

Aardwolf

Right front

Right back

- Have narrow tracks that lack angled back pad; toe pads large and close to small main pads.
- Live in family units, but forage alone.
- Wide habitat range dictated by availability of food.

Length (average)	
Front	60 mm
Back	53 mm

Honey badger

Right front
(in soft ground)

Right back
(in soft ground)

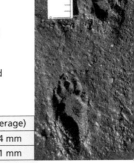

- Large, robust, clawed tracks; claws on front feet are up to 25 mm long. Pads shown in grey tend to show only in mud or soft sand.
- Solitary forager.
- Most habitats.

Length (average)	
Front	54 mm
Back	81 mm

Porcupine

Right front
(in soft ground)

Right back (full sole of foot)

- Tracks similar to those of honey badgers, but much shorter claw marks on front feet; only four toe impressions usually show in front, while all pads usually show in hind tracks.
- Solitary foragers.
- Nearly all habitats.

Length (average)	
Front	70 mm
Back	80 mm

African civet

Right front

Right back

- Could be confused with tracks of small dogs, but back edge of main pads are slightly concave (straight in dogs); toe pads large and close to main pad.
- Solitary foragers.
- Open woodland and thickets near water.

Length (average)	
Front	50 mm
Back	48 mm

Black-backed jackal

Right front

Right back

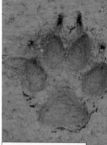

- Hind tracks are smaller than front, with prominent triangular main pads; four toe pads on front and back feet. Clawmarks always visible.
- Solitary, pairs and small groups.
- Widespread.

Length (average)	
Front	54 mm
Back	43 mm

Bat-eared fox

Right front

Right back

- Tracks smaller than those of jackals; front clawmarks are up to 18 mm ahead of tracks; main pads are often obscured by dense underfoot hair.
- Family parties of 3–6 animals.
- Favour open country with low scrub.

Length (average)	
Front	39 mm
Back	36 mm

Cape fox

Right front

Right back

- Tracks similar to those of bat-eared foxes, but more frequently obscured by dense underfoot hair between pads.
- Solitary foragers.
- Southern African endemics in the drier west; occupy areas of open grassland and scrub.
- Farmland.

Length (average)	
Front	38 mm
Back	36 mm

White-tailed mongoose

Right front

Right back

- Could be mistaken for small jackal tracks, but toe pad impressions are smaller.
- Solitary foragers.
- Woodland savanna.

Length (average)	
Front	45 mm
Back	41 mm

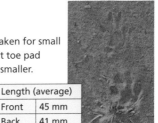

Water mongoose

Right front

Right back

- Four elongated toe impressions usually show in each track; rarely, a fifth is visible.
- Solitary and linear range.
- Rivers, lakes, dams.

Length (average)	
Front	46 mm
Back	36 mm

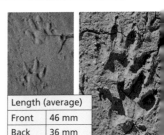

Banded mongoose

Right front

Right back

- Only four (of five) toe imprints usually show in each track.
- Live in troops of 5–30, or more.
- Woodland savanna.

Length (average)	
Front	29 mm
Back	29 mm

Yellow mongoose

Right front

Right back

- Tiny, dog-like tracks; fairly robust but short claws on tracks.
- Live in colonies, but hunt alone.
- Grassland, scrub – only in southern Africa.

Length (average)	
Front	26 mm
Back	25 mm

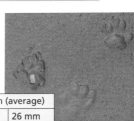

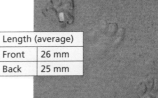

23

Right front

Right back

Suricate (Meerkat)

- Tracks similar to those of yellow mongooses (they may occur together), but claws on front tracks are especially long (>15 mm).
- Social.
- Only in southern Africa; favour open, dry country.

Length (average)	
Front	24 mm
Back	23 mm

Right front

Right back

Small grey mongoose

- They have five toes on each foot, but usually only four show in tracks.
- Solitary.
- Occupies most habitats in range, from forest to scrub.
- Only in southern Africa

Length (average)	
Front	26 mm
Back	25 mm

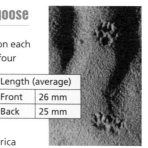

Right front

Right back

Slender mongoose

- Tracks similar to small grey mongooses, but main pads marginally larger and ranges barely overlap.
- Solitary.
- Habitats range from forest to savanna.

Length (average)	
Front	25 mm
Back	22 mm

Right front

Right back

Striped polecat

- Five toe pads usually visible in tracks, compared to four of mongooses.
- Solitary foragers.
- All habitats.

Length (average)	
Front	22 mm
Back	22 mm

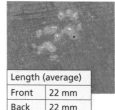

Hands & feet

All of the primates, including humans, fall into the 'hands and feet' category, as do Cape clawless otters and hyraxes (dassies). Apart from the hand- and foot-like appearance of these tracks, they are characterized by the absence of claw (nail) marks showing in any of the tracks. Only very rarely have we found nail marks left in fine, soft river silt (from savanna baboon and vervet monkey) in the form of fine, slightly curved lines just ahead of the toe tracks. Unlike human footprints, where the big toe is parallel to the other toes, in other primates, the big toe stands out at an angle.

Savanna baboon

Right front

Right back

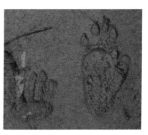

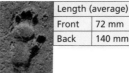

- Of the non-human 'hands and feet' tracks in the region, those of baboons are largest. Handprints show fully extended fingers, and back toe extends at about 45 degrees.
- Live in troops of 15–100 animals.
- Many habitats.

Length (average)	
Front	72 mm
Back	140 mm

Vervet monkey

Right front

Right back

- Tracks similar to, but smaller than, those of baboons; fingers are extended, and back toe at roughly 45 degrees.
- Live in troops of up to 20 or more individuals.
- Wooded savanna, riverine woodland, even extending into arid areas.

Length (average)	
Front	55 mm
Back	85 mm

Cape clawless otter

Right front

Right back

- Primate-like footprints with five toe imprints, but on harder ground only four may show; grey area in front track may only show in soft ground.
- Mainly solitary.
- Along rivers, lakes, marshes, dams and beaches.

Length (average)	
Front	70 mm
Back	100 mm

Greater galagos (Bushbabies)

Right front

Right back

- Large big toe, in particular, stands out at right angle to foot, other round toe prints are tightly clustered.
- Spend much time moving about and foraging on ground.
- Forest, woodland and river margins.

Length (average)	
Front	50 mm
Back	80 mm

Rock hyrax (Dassie)

Right front

Right back

- Four stubby toes on front feet, three on back feet; curved claw on back feet rarely shows in track.
- Best identified as four-track clusters, similar to hares and rabbits (p. 28).
- Live in groups.
- Rocky habitats.

Length (average)	
Front	40 mm
Back	50 mm

Non-cloven hooves

Unlike cloven-hooved mammals that have two (more or less) evenly shaped and sized hoof halves (one at the base of each toe), non-cloven-hooved mammals have a single horny sheath capping the tip of the 'third' toe. The leading edge of the front, non-cloven hoof is rounded; the anterior edge of the back may be rounded or squared, and may vary within a single species. The best-known members of this group are the domestic horse and donkey. If one examines the underside of a hoof, one sees a hard, horny outer rim that takes most of the stress, wear and tear, plus an inner softer sole with a triangular section, known as the 'frog'.

Plains & Burchell's zebras

Right front

Right back

- Tracks resemble those of small horses, with hind tracks more elongated than front.
- Live in small family groups; may form large herds in some areas.
- Grassed plains.

Plains zebra track on hard ground

Length (average)	
Front	130 mm
Back	130 mm

Mountain zebra

Right front

Right back

- Similar to tracks of plains zebra, but narrower and more like those of donkeys.
- Live in small family herds.
- Open hill and grassland country; extreme west and southwest. Not found in East Africa.

Length (average)	
Front	120 mm
Back	120 mm

Clusters

Species in this group are most easily identified by a full cluster of the four track imprints of one animal, rather than the track left by a single foot. In nearly all cases where only a single footprint is found, identification can prove very difficult.

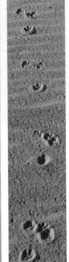

Hares & rabbits

Total length of 300 mm

Left back   Right back

Right front

Left front

- When moving rapidly, tracks of hind feet always placed ahead of front feet.
- Solitary.
- Most habitats.

Ground squirrels

Right front

Right back

- Front tracks are close together and paired; hind tracks also paired, but wider-spread and ahead of front.
- Arid, open areas.

Length (average)	
Front	22 mm (full)
Back	60 mm (full)

Other species

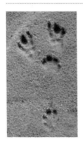

Apart from hares, rabbits and ground squirrels, similar paw clusters can be identified in the tree squirrels, gerbils (below) and hyraxes (left). See also 'Hands & feet' for hyraxes (p. 26).

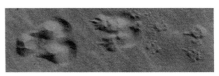

Three toes

Other than birds, only three mammal species clearly fall within this group: the aardvark and the two springhare species. The aardvark has four toes on the front foot and five toes on the hind foot, but usually only three toes show clearly on each track, except on very soft ground. The much smaller springhare moves in a jumping motion and only on hind legs; although there are four toes on the hind foot, usually only three leave track impressions. Front feet are not used in locomotion.

Aardvark

Right front

Right back

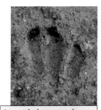

- Usually only three toe imprints show clearly on each track. Each toe has a large, heavy nail: those on the front feet are most strongly developed and are used for digging burrows and excavating termite mounds (for food).
- Solitary.

Length (average)	
Front	100 mm (with claws)
Back	90 mm (with claws)

Springhare

Hopping tracks – toes only

Sitting tracks – both hind feet

Left back   Right back

- On the move, they bound on hind feet only. When moving rapidly, only three toe tips and their diamond-shaped claws touch the ground. When sitting, full length of feet leave track impressions.
- Loose colonies.
- Open grassland.

Length (average)	
Toes	38 mm
Full foot	102 mm

Bird tracks: webbed

Tracks from birds with webbed feet are quite frequently found, as their association with water means that their feet come into contact with wet substrates, such as silt, mud and damp sand – ideal tracking mediums. Many swimming birds, such as cormorants, gulls, pelicans, ducks and geese have webbed feet. All have three forward-pointing toes, with most having a small, unwebbed, back-pointing toe; cormorants and pelicans have a relatively long hind toe that is also linked by webbing. In all cases, claws are relatively short and may not always show in the track.

Pelicans

● Pelicans, of which there are two species in the regions, have by far the largest webbed feet and leave distinctive 'pigeon-toed' tracks.
● Depending on the substrate, the webbing may or may not show in the tracks. Tracks in the left image were in relatively coarse silt/sand and no webbing is evident. Pelican tracks are similar to those of cormorants.

Flamingos

● Clear individual tracks of either greater or lesser flamingos are often difficult to locate, as they usually forage in large flocks.
● Tracks are clearly semi-circular with no back toe marks.

Geese

● The deep-set track of a Spurwing goose (far right) in fine, damp silt clearly shows webbing and the short, angled back toe mark. Egyptian Goose (right).

Gulls

● This track is from a Cape gull. The short back toe often does not show in tracks; here, webbing and claw marks are clear. All gulls have similar track structures.

Cormorants

● This group is tied to marine or freshwater habitats. They often perch on rocks and in trees, but tracks may be found on beaches and estuary mud banks. Often only three forward-pointing toes show in tracks, with the fourth usually visible only in fine sand or wet silt. They are often in flocks, so many tracks will be present.

Penguin

● African penguins have three stout, forward-pointing toes and a rear toe-like extension. As with other web-footed birds, webbing does not often show clearly in the track. Restricted to coastal southern Africa.

Bird tracks: not webbed

This type of track encompasses most species of bird, the majority of which have three toes pointing forward and one toe pointing backward, as indicated below (a); next, the herons and egrets with an offset back toe (b); then, most game birds with three toes forward and one short back-angled toe (c); and finally, three-toed track impressions (d) include bustards, thick-knees and plovers.

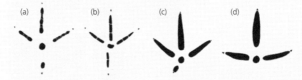

Cranes

● Four crane species occur in the regions, with the blue crane being the most widespread in the south; three forward-pointing toes show in their tracks, but not the back toe.

Bustards

● All bustards and korhaans have just three stout, forward-pointing toes and no back toe, although the 'heel pad' may resemble short back toe in tracks.

Secretarybird

● The tracks of this large 'ground eagle' resemble those of the bustards and korhaans, but the short, angled back toe (and its claw) usually leaves a mark in the tracks (far right). A short stretch of their walking trail (right) shows a substantial stride.

Herons & egrets

● Herons, egrets
and egrets have
characteristic feet: three
long forward-pointing
toes and a long hind toe,
but the latter is usually
slightly off-set (shown
bottom right). However,
in some circumstances
the back toe may appear
to be in line with the
central front toe within
the same trail, indicating
flexibility.

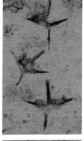

Guineafowl

● The two guineafowl species and the many
spurfowl and francolin species in the region
have similarly structured feet, with three
robust, forward-pointing toes and a very
short, inward-angled back toe. Although the
latter nearly always shows in their tracks,
it may be absent on hard substrates. All
species usually occur in flocks or coveys of
2–20 or more, depending on the species.

Hornbills

● All hornbills have similar feet: three
closely-aligned, forward-pointing toes
and one straight, backward-pointing toe.
They may walk, but the smaller species
may also hop, as did the red-billed
hornbill that created these tracks (right).
Hornbills are common and widespread
in both regions and are often associated
with conservation area camps.

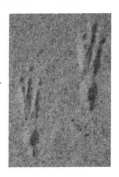

Doves & pigeons

● All doves and pigeons leave a 'pigeon-toed' trail, with the middle toe on each foot pointing slightly inwards. This can be clearly seen in the three trails below. Tracks of the different species are difficult to tell apart – use range maps and habitat to aid identification.

Plovers & lapwings

● Plovers and lapwings, as well as many wading birds, leave distinctive tracks: three forward-pointing toes with the back toe lacking.

● Many passerines leave both walking and hopping trails, such as the **Karoo thrush** (left); a partial hopping trail of this thrush is shown at far left. Hopping and walking gaits may alternate.

Owls & ostrich

- Several groups of bird species have two forward-pointing and two backward-pointing toes, e.g. owls, woodpeckers and parrots.
- Ostriches have just two forward-pointing toes.

- The foot structure (right) of the spotted eagle-owl is typical of all owls, with two forward-pointing and two backward-pointing toes (each armed with a long, sharp claw). The spotted eagle-owl tracks (above left) clearly show their toe layout; the inner back toe frequently stands out at a 90-degree angle. **Note:** Claws have made clear marks in the track, with drag from back claw.

- Ostriches, the world's largest flightless birds, have distinctive two-toed feet (left). One large toe is armed with a heavy, curved claw; the other is a much smaller, outer toe, with a small claw that seldom shows in tracks. The walking track of an ostrich, clearly showing the large toe, claw and smaller outer toe, can be seen at far left. Ostriches occur in many conservation areas and on farms.

Tramline-like trails

Tramline-like trails with dragmark

● These trails and tracks are characterized by sets of footprints to the right and left of a tail drag. Animals in this group include various lizards, Nile crocodiles and scorpions, amongst others. With the exception of crocodiles and monitor lizards, identification to species level is rarely possible.

● **Lizard trails** often show a central drag mark left by the tail (above).
● Although **scorpions** (right) usually move with the tail curved over the back, sometimes it leaves a drag between the foot imprints.
● **Cape fur seal** tracks (left) have a substantial central drag mark made by the body and flippers. Found on southern African shores.

Right Front

Right Back

Nile crocodile

● Front tracks usually show a five-toe impression; back tracks have only four toes.
● Their tail may drag heavily, leaving a substantial trail, or be lifted off the ground with only the tip occasionally leaving a mark.

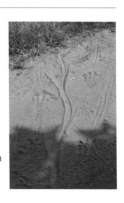

Tramline-like trails without dragmark

● The tramline-like trails without a dragmark are indicative of tortoises, terrapins, frogs, crabs and many other invertebrates.

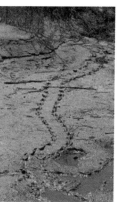 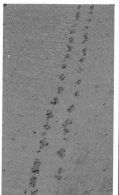 

● **Tortoise** and **terrapin** tracks (above) form classic tramline-like trails, with the feet on the right and left evenly spaced. Clear foot imprints are relatively rare, as these reptiles tend to drag their feet; this is particulary obvious at top right. Tortoises and terrapins occur widely in both regions, but are absent from the Namib Desert.

● Many **insects** leave typical tramline-like trails (left). However, it is usually very difficult to identify which species created this type of track.

● **Toads** hop and walk; when hopping, they leave distinctive four-cluster patterns (right). In this example, the long hind-foot tracks lie at the bottom of each cluster, with the small front tracks at the top.

Undulating trails

Undulating tracks are left by many snakes, legless lizards, some golden moles and a wide range of insect species. However, it is those of the snakes that are probably best known. Even on relatively smooth surfaces, most **snakes** are able to gain sufficient traction by moving the body in a serpentine motion, pushing against the ground with the sides of the body (above); this is not always so obvious, as can be seen in the images below (left and middle). Unless the snake is actually seen moving along a trail, it is virtually impossible to identify the species involved. Although most **legless lizards** live a subterranean life, they occasionally move along the surface (below right). Their tracks are indistinguishable from those of small snakes.

● A few species of snake, such as **pythons** and **adders**, when undisturbed and travelling at leisure, move in a more or less straight line (left). The tail tip often leaves a central drag line.

● Several species of **golden mole** occur in the regions, leaving meandering foraging trails just under the surface (right). Depending on the species, they may be located in coastal dunes and even just above the high tide mark, as well as in gardens and along forest edges.

● There are many insects that leave undulating and winding trails, which may indicate feeding actions, such as those of **wood-boring beetle** larvae (below left) or the foraging trails of ants (below right). Many **ant and termite** species have central colonies, from which radiate numerous trails that lead to feeding grounds; some of these trail complexes may cover many hundreds of metres.

Watch for ...

In parts of southern and East Africa, tracks may be attributable to domesticated mammals, even in conservation areas. Dog tracks can be mistaken for jackals and hyaenas. Domesticated cat tracks can be confused with wild cats, though wild cat tracks are larger. Cattle tracks may resemble buffalo or eland tracks, and horse tracks may resemble zebra tracks. The 'squared' tracks of sheep and goats are not likely to be confused with those of antelope, though they may resemble pigs tracks.

Dog

Right front

Right back

Cat

Right front

Right back

Cattle

Right front

Right back

Horse

Right front

Right back

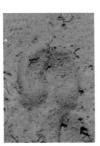

Sheep

Right front

Right back

Goat

Right front

Right back